# JUDGE DREDD

# INTRODUCTION

This is the third collection of artist Cam Kennedy's work on *Judge Dredd* and it shows that he's just as adept at playing up the humorous aspects of the story as he is at dramatising the action.

*The Secret Diary of Adrian Cockroach*, originally scrawled within the pages of *2000 AD* Prog 458, was inspired by Adrian Mole's diary of adolescent angst as related by Sue Townsend. Writers John Wagner and Alan Grant were reflecting upon what Adrian Mole might be like if he were a resident of Mega-City One. After a little playing about with the name, they decided he'd be a cockroach – *Aged 13½*, though, younger than the Mole's 13¾.

*The Falucci Tape* first played in Progs 461-463 but the character of Herman the Kneepad Kid had made his debut three years earlier in a story written by Alan Grant for the *1984 Judge Dredd Annual*. Grant and Wagner's premise for the present story was the idea that a chance encounter with a Judge might turn an apparently normal citizen into the twisted individual we find here. Herman is arrested by Judge Sladek on the grounds that he looks suspicious. He has to spend six hours filling out a form that delves into every aspect of his life, including a psychological profile. In the course of this ordeal, he has to report misdemeanors committed by his parents, for which they're still serving sentences.

Judge Dredd's home turf of Mega-City One is located on the post-holocaust Eastern Seaboard of America, so it's somehow very apt that the final stories in this volume should have been prompted by contact with comic companies situated on the present day East Coast.

*The Big Sleep* began with Cam Kennedy's character sketches of a figure on a sky-sled for a series which he, Wagner and Grant were creating for DC Comics. The editorial staff at DC felt that the character didn't fit the tone of the series, claiming that he looked more like something from Judge Dredd. Not wanting to let an idea go to waste, Wagner and Grant decided to fly their figure on a skysled into *2000 AD* Progs 466-467. On the journey, the sled's occupant became Flip Marlowe, Intimidator by trade. Along with the story title, Marlowe's name and terse dialogue were derived from the works of celebrated crime writer, Raymond Chandler.

As the more astute of you will realise, *The Art of Kenny Who?* (Progs 477-479) stars Cam Kennedy's self-caricature. The story sprang from communication problems Wagner and Grant were having with an American publisher regarding a story placed there. They arranged for Kennedy to draw the series, hoping to spark a little more enthusiasm from across the Atlantic. A phone call to the company announcing the artist garnered the response "Cam Kenny Who?" Eventually Kennedy visited the USA to discuss the project in person. This story was written while he was away, with Wagner and Grant exaggerating the problems of dealing with 'Big One'.

It should be noted that Judge Dredd's participation in these stories is minimal (although he's at his belligerent best when he does appear), and it's a tribute to the scope of Mega-City One and to the strips creators that this can occur without giving the readers a Mega-loss of thrill-power.

**Frank Plowright,** *April 1987.*

*JOHN WAGNER was largely responsible, along with Pat Mills, for the renaissance of British comics in the 1970s and the creation of* Battle, Action *and* 2000 AD. *He has scripted* Strontium Dog, Robo-Hunter *and* Judge Dredd *under his pseudonyms and is currently working with Alan Grant, co-writing* Judge Dredd *for IPC and* The Outcasts *for DC. He is also developing* The Last American, *with Mike McMahon for Marvel's Epic Comics line.*

*ALAN GRANT began his comics career in 1977, writing* Tarzan *for European publication. After a year as sub-editor on* 2000 AD *he went freelance, and since 1980 has worked in partnership with John Wagner. Current stories include:* Judge Dredd, Strontium Dog *and* Ace Trucking Co *for* 2000 AD; Kaleb Daark, *with Brett Ewins, for Citadel Miniatures;* Outcasts *with Cam Kennedy, for D.C.;* The Last American, *with Mike McMahon, for Epic.*

*CAM KENNEDY worked on the* Commando *books from 1960-1972 for DC Thompson. After a six year stint as a painter in Normandy he returned to the comics medium working on* Battle *for IPC. Among his most popular strips were* War Dog, Fighting Man *and* Clash of the Gods. *This was followed in 1980 by work for* 2000 AD *the* VC's, Rogue Trooper *and* Judge Dredd. *He is currently drawing* The Outcasts *for DC Comics.*

Published by Titan Books Ltd, 58 St Giles High St, London WC2H 8LH, England. Distributed in the United Kingdom and the United States of America by Titan Distributors Ltd, P.O. Box 250, London E3 4RT, England. *Judge Dredd* is © IPC Magazines Ltd, 1987. This edition is © Titan Books Ltd, 1987. Printed in England. ISBN 1 85286 001 4. *First edition August 1987.*

10  9  8  7  6  5  4  3  2  1

# THE ART OF KENNY WHO?.

THE **10.00 ZOOM** FROM THE **CALEDONIAN HAB ZONE** CLEARS THE **ATLANTIC TUNNEL** AT PRECISELY 08.45 MEGA-CITY TIME —

ALL PASSENGERS PROCEED TO **IMMIGRATION** CONTROL. HAVE YOUR DOCUMENTS AND MEDICAL CERTIFICATES READY. FAILURE TO DO SO MAY BE AN OFFENCE.

NO LOITERING IN THE FEEDWAY. KEEP MOVING.

HAVE ALL HANDLUGGAGE READY FOR INSPECTION.

TWELVE HOURS HE'S BEEN TRAVELLING. TIRED, WASHED OUT, AND THE **ZOOMLAG** ISN'T HELPING.

# JUDGE DREDD

Script T B GROVER
Art CAM KENNEDY
Lettering T FRAME

STILL, HE'S HERE. HE'S MORTGAGED HIS PAD, SOLD HIS POD. BUT IT'LL BE WORTH IT. THIS IS WHERE **THE FUTURE** LIES.

I'M HERE AT LAST — AND THERE'S NO STOPPING ME NOW!

**KENNY WHO?**, HUH? THIS YOUR REAL NAME?

YES SIR.

PURPOSE OF VISIT?

I'M LOOKING FOR WORK.

**WORK?** WE GOT 98 PER CENT UNEMPLOYMENT HERE. WHAT MAKES YOU THINK YOU'VE GOT ANYTHING **WE** WANT, **WHO?**?

I... I'M AN **ARTIST.**

ARTIST SCHMARTIST! SO WHAT? WE GOT PLENTY **ROBOTS** TO DRAW OUR PICTURES.

I'M **BETTER** THAN ANY ROBOT, JUDGE! I'VE GOT SOMETHING THEY CAN NEVER HAVE — **TALENT!**

BETTER HAVE A LOOK AT THIS, DREDD.

THIS **YOU**, WHO??

YES, SIR. IT'S MY PORTFOLIO. MY BEST WORK.

WELL I DON'T LIKE IT!

BU-BU-BUT WHY?

'COS IT'S **FREAK-OUT, WEIRDO** STUFF, THAT'S WHY!

HELL! **BIG 1** CLOSE AT FOUR! ONLY TWENTY MINUTES – I'LL NEVER MAKE IT!

STEP ON IT, DRIVER!

I'LL DO THE DRIVIN', BUB.

YELLA-CAB

850 833

FOUR O!

STOP! DON'T CLOSE – WAIT FOR ME!

CLUNGGG!!!

LET ME IN! YOU CAN'T DO THIS TO ME!

BIG 1

I'M AN ARTIST, DAMMIT – AN **ARTIST**!

NEXT PROG: **WHO'S WHO??**

# THE ART OF KENNY WHO?.

ARTIST KENNY WHO? HAS MORTGAGED HIS ALL TO COME TO MEGA-CITY ONE IN SEARCH OF THE FAME HIS TALENT DESERVES —

PLEASE, DON'T CLOSE! YOU'VE GOT TO LET ME IN! I'VE ONLY GOT A 24 HOUR PERMIT! I CAN'T COME BACK IN THE MORNING!

SCRIPT T B GROVER
ART CAM KENNEDY
LETTERING T FRAME

PLEASE...!

SOB!

STENNESS HARRIER

WHAT? WHO?.

THAT'S WHAT I'M ASKING YOU. WHO? IS MY NAME.

NO — YOU SHOULD SAY "WHAT" IS MY NAME.

NO! WHO?! KENNY WHO?...I'M KENNY WHO?.

I'M TELLING YOU, I DON'T KNOW!

MY CARD.

KENNY WHO?

I SEE!

WELL YOU JUST SIT THERE AND DRINK YOUR CAF, KENNY, WHILE I LOOK THROUGH YOUR PORTFOLIO.

KENNY WHO? SITS BACK AND SIPS HIS STEAMING BREW — AND DREAMS OF THE FAME AND FORTUNE THAT SURELY AWAIT HIM.

KENNY! WAKE UP!

HUH? WHAT?

NO — WHO?! HA HA! I THOUGHT WE'D GOT THAT SETTLED.

GOSH — SEVEN O! MUST'VE DOZED OFF!

SO WHAT DO YOU THINK OF MY DRAWINGS?

I'M SORRY, KENNY...

YOU — YOU DIDN'T LIKE THEM?

I'M AFRAID NOT.

BUT THEY'RE GOOD! I KNOW IT!

OH, IN PARTS. AN ANGLE HERE — A LINE THERE. BUT IT'S NOTHING A COMPETENT ROBOT COULDN'T HANDLE, IN A THOUSANDTH OF THE TIME.

I'LL BE FRANK WITH YOU, KENNY. ART'S A TOUGH GAME THESE DAYS. NOT MANY HUMANS EVER MAKE IT. THEY'VE GOT TO HAVE SOMETHING... TRULY SPECIAL. REAL TALENT. AND YOU, KENNY, JUST DON'T MAKE THE GRADE.

TAKE MY ADVICE. GO BACK TO CAL HAB. FIND OUT WHERE YOUR TALENTS REALLY LIE. BUILDING WALLS, PERHAPS.

# CLUNGGG

BOIL'S HEAD

ANOTHER TRIPLE RIPPLE, PAL!

HAPPY JUICE NOW

HEY! ANYBODY WANNA ARM WRESHLE?

COOL IT, MISTER! YOU'LL HAVE THE JUDGES IN!

THE BOIL'S HEAD A GOOD SPOT TO SQUEEZE IN

IT'S NOT EASY FOR A MAN WHOSE DREAM DIES. TO HAVE BELIEVED IN HIMSELF — IN HIS TALENT, HIS ART — FOR SO LONG...THEN TO HAVE HIS OWN INABILITY THRUST BRUTALLY IN HIS FACE.

TALENT! HE KNOWS NOW WHAT A SHAM IT'S ALL BEEN! HOW COULD HE HAVE DELUDED HIMSELF ALL THIS TIME? HOW?

AN ARTISHT — RUBBISH! I'M NOBODY. KENNY... KENNY NOBODY...

...AND FINALLY TONIGHT ON "THE VIZ ARTS" — NEWS FROM BIG 1 ABOUT A MAJOR NEW TALENT POISED TO EXPLODE ONTO THE MEGA-CITY TRASHZINE SCENE.

THE VIZ ARTS

DREDD

THESE POWERFUL STUDIES OF THE CITY'S FOREMOST ACTION MAN AMPLY DEMONSTRATE A TALENT BOTH UNIQUE AND DRAMATIC.

TAKE IT FROM THIS REVIEWER, BIG 1'S NEW ART ROBOT JIMMY WHO? IS SET TO BE THE BIG NAME IN TRASHART FOR MANY YEARS TO COME.

HUH? JIMMY WHO??

DON'T ASHK ME, FRIEND. DIDN'T CATCH IT MYSHELF.

THOSE DRAWINGS... THE STYLE — THE COMPOSITION — IT'S **ME**.

'SH JUDGE DRUDGE.

THE PICTURES ON THE SCREEN BRING KENNY WHO? ABRUPTLY TO HIS SENSES —

YOU DON'T UNDERSTAND — THEY'RE **MINE**! I DREW THEM! BUT...

...BUT I **DIDN'T** DRAW THEM!

SOUNDSH LIKE ITSH TIME TO GO HOME, BUDDY.

BIG 1 HAS STOLEN MY **TALENT**!

HEY, COME BACK WITH THAT!

INTERESHTING FELLA.

A **RED RAGE** GRIPS KENNY WHO? AS HE RUNS ACROSS THE PLAZA —

# THE ART OF KENNY WHO?.

On Mega-City One in search of fame, Britto artist **KENNY WHO?** has had his talent stolen by **BIG1** publishing.

ALAN DONALDSON BLOCK

SCRIPT
T B GROVER
ART
CAM KENNEDY
LETTERING
T FRAME

JIMMY WHO??
I'M AFRAID I
DON'T —

LIAR! YOU KNOW! I DON'T KNOW
HOW YOU DID IT BUT YOU **STOLE** MY
**TALENT!** AN' YOU EVEN HAD THE
CHEEK TO STEAL MY **NAME** AS WELL!

I'M GONNA ASK YOU
ONE MORE TIME —
AN' YOU BETTER COME
CLEAN OR YOU AND YOUR
HEAD ARE GOING TO BE
APPLYING FOR **SEVERANCE PAY** —

WHERE'S **JIMMY-FLAMIN'-WHO??**

SOMETHING IN **KENNY WHO?**'S EYES — AND
SOMETHING **ELSE** IN HIS RAZOR SHARP **AXE** —
CONVINCES THE SENIOR EDITOR. . .

OKAY, 'NUFF SAID.
IT'S TRUTH-TELLIN'
TIME, TIGER !

COME WITH ME.

BIG 1 BULLPEN

MEET OUR **ARTISTS**.

JUST FLIPPIN' **BOXES**!

OH, FAR MORE THAN THAT!

SCRIPTS ARE FED IN DIRECTLY FROM OUR **REHASH** BANKS UPSTAIRS.

THE ART ROBOTS CAN DRAW IN ANY STYLE — IN LINE, WASH, HALF-TONE, COLOUR — YOU NAME IT.

PAGES COME OUT IN LESS THAN A MINUTE, ALL FULLY-LETTERED, OF COURSE.

**THAT'S** NOT **ART**!

BUT IT'S **CHEAP**!

BUT WHY ME? YOU SAID MY WORK WAS NO GOOD.

A LITTLE WHITE LIE, KENNY. IN FACT, IT WAS **BRILLIANT**. A MAJOR NEW TALENT IF EVER I SAW ONE. QUITE **UNIQUE**...

...AT LEAST, YOU **WERE**. YOU SEE, YOU MADE THE MISTAKE OF DOZING OFF. ZOOMLAGGED, I SUPPOSE. UNDERSTANDABLE.

SO I TOOK THE LIBERTY OF FEEDING YOUR PORTFOLIO INTO ONE OF OUR MACHINES. WITH ENOUGH INPUT THEY CAN MIMIC **ANY** STYLE.

KENNY WHO? — MEET JIMMY WHO?.

COMPOUNDING HIS STRING OF CRIMES HE STEALS A **POWERBOARD** FROM COMPANY STORES.

HIS ONLY CHANCE IS TO FLEE THE CITY BEFORE HE IS REPORTED.

THE **ATLANTIC TUNNEL!** I'LL CATCH THE **MIDNIGHT ZOOM!** I CAN MAKE IT!

IMMIGRATION

JUSTICE DEPARTMENT! I WANT TO REPORT A **MURDER**...

THE MURDER OF A **GREAT TALENT!**

THERE'S NOTHING UNUSUAL ABOUT A MAN RUNNING TO CATCH A ZOOM, YET THE KEEN EYES OF THE SENIOR JUDGE ON DUTY ARE DRAWN TO KENNY WHO? LIKE A MAGNET.

YOU!

IMMIGRATION

**WHO?**, ISN'T IT?

YES, SIR.

LEAVIN' EARLY, ARE YOU? BUSINESS A SUCCESS?

NO, SIR. THEY DON'T WANT ARTISTS HERE. NOT **REAL** ARTISTS.

I TOLD YOU THAT THIS MORNING.

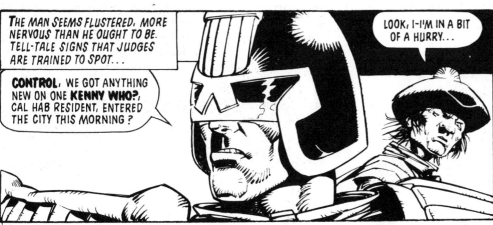

THE MAN SEEMS FLUSTERED. MORE NERVOUS THAN HE OUGHT TO BE. TELL-TALE SIGNS THAT JUDGES ARE TRAINED TO SPOT...

CONTROL, WE GOT ANYTHING NEW ON ONE KENNY WHO?, CAL HAB RESIDENT, ENTERED THE CITY THIS MORNING?

LOOK, I-I'M IN A BIT OF A HURRY...

AFFIRMATIVE! CALL JUST CAME IN — CREEP RAN AMOK AT BIG 1. GOT HIM ON B&E, GBH, MALICIOUS DAMAGE, ASSAULT WITH A DEADLY WEAPON — MORE CHARGES TO FOLLOW.

WHO?! HOLD IT!

WHO?

WHO?

C'MON, LEGS, YOU CAN DO IT!

EASTBOUND ZOOM 11-53

WALK

HE'S GOING TO MAKE THE ZOOM. CAN'T GET A CLEAR SHOT.

RICOCHET!

SPTANNG!

SPTANNGGG!

KNEEPAD'S GONE REAL MEAN SINCE THE JUDGES PICKED HIM UP ON SUS. I MEAN, SIX LOUSY HOURS, MAN, AN' HE DIDN'T DO NOTHIN'. THAT'S ENOUGH TO TURN ANY GUY.

UNNFFF!

CRAK·K·K!

CREMOLA! YOU'VE HURT HIM BAD, KNEE!

GINK HURT HISSELF. SHOULDN'TA FELL LIKE THAT.

WHAT'S HE GOT, SONNY?

USUAL DREKK. FIFTY CASH — REST'S ALL PLASTIC.

AND THIS...

JUST A TAPE SLUG.

CHEAPSKATE GINK! TOLD YA HE WASN'T WORTH TAPPIN'!

SO ANYWAY, WE BEAT IT. AIN'T TOO SMART TO HANG AROUND A POTENTIAL STIFF...

...ESPECIALLY WHEN YOU HEAR A JUDGE'S LAWMASTER APPROACHING.

TAP VICTIM.

OR WAS.

DREDD TO CONTROL! WE GOT ONE FOR THE MEAT WAGON, SKED ROW. NAME OF **SELWYN FALUCCI**, APARTMENT 1804, DEREK HATTON BLOCK.

DEFINITE TAP VICTIM. BETTER SEND FORENSIC DOWN AS WELL.

PERPS PROBABLY LONG GONE. I'LL CHECK FALUCCI'S APARTMENT.

WE PICKED UP A COUPLA SYNTHI-PIZZAS AN' A TEN-PACK AND HEADED BACK TO DIRTY JOHN'S MOPAD.

84 CREDS, SON.

PIZZA HOVEL

THAT'S MORE'N WE STOLE!

CRAKK!

WHISTLE FOR IT, ELDO!

26

'COURSE KNEEPAD WANTED TO SEND THE SLUG STRAIGHT TO THE JUDGES. HE HATED THAT **SLYDOG** LIKE CRAZY.

CONTROL! I'M IN THE FALUCCI APARTMENT. GOT SOME SORT OF RADIO MONITORING DEVICE IN HERE. SEND UP A TEK SQUAD.

JUDGES AIN'T ALLOWED TO HAVE GIRLFRIENDS, SEE. JUSTICE DEPT GET ONE WHIFF OF YOLANDA BABY AN' SLYDOG'S OFF THE FORCE. LIKE HIS FEET DON'T TOUCH THE GROUND, MAN!

DON'T BE DUMB, KNEE! THERE'S **CREDS** IN THIS!

LONG AS WE GOT THIS, SLYDOG SLADEK BELONGS TO US! WE SAY JUMP, HE JUMPS — OR WE SEND IT STRAIGHT TO THE CHIEF CHEEZ!

BLACKMAIL! YOU BETCHA!

NEXT PROG: **THE SQUEEZE!**

ONCE ME AN' KNEEPAD AN' DIRTY JOHN HAD DECIDED ON BLACKMAILING SLYDOG SLADEK, WE HAD TO FIGURE THE BEST WAY OF GOING ABOUT IT.

HELLO, JUSTICE CENTRAL...?

I MEAN, YOU DON'T JUST PED UP TO A JUDGE IN THE STREET AN' SAY: HEY, LAWMAN, I GOT A TAPE SLUG OF YOUR BIG LOVE SCENE WITH YOUR SECRET POOPSIE!

WANNA SPEAK TO JUDGE SLADEK.

SLADEK'S UNAVAILABLE. WHAT'S YOUR PROBLEM, CITIZEN?

IT'S JUST BETWEEN ME AN' SLADEK. LISTEN, GIVE HIM A MESSAGE...

TELL HIM TO MEET ME IN ONE HOUR, CORNER OF BONAR AN' SKED. TELL HIM I GOT SOME VERY IMPORTANT INFO.

WHAT'S YOUR NAME, CITIZEN?

KLIK!

NO NAMES.

RECKON HE'LL SHOW, SONNY?

HE BETTER, IF HE KNOWS WHAT'S GOOD FOR HIM.

OL' KNEEPAD, HE'S CRAZY, MAN. I MEAN, HERE WE ARE WITH A GENUINE JUDGE IN OUR POCKETS AN' HE'S STILL KNEEIN' PAY PHONES.

CHINNGG!

GUESS OLD HABITS DIE HARD.

34

HE COULD BOOK ME – **SHOOT** ME, EVEN!

**RELAX**, DIRT! HE DON'T DARE! 'COS WE'RE SITTIN' HERE WITH THE TAPE, RIGHT?

SLYDOG DOES EXACTLY WHAT HE'S TOLD OR IT GOES TO THE CHIEF CHEEZ AN' HE'S STREETMEAT.

YEAH... I GUESS...

NOW YOU KNOW WHAT YOU GOTTA SAY?

YEAH, YEAH. WIRED TO MY BRAIN.

GO GET HIM, DIRTY!

SO THERE'S ME AN' KNEEPAD, ALREADY COUNTIN' THE CREDS. I MEAN, THIS WAS PRIMO SCAMMO, MAN. WE HAD THAT JUDGE BY THE MAIN ZIP AN' WE WAS GONNA HOLD ON TILL HIS EYES WATERED.

LITTLE DID WE KNOW DIRTY JOHN WOULDN'T BE COMIN' BACK.

NEXT PROG: **THE PRICE OF LOVE!**

YOUR EX-HUSBAND HAD RECORDING EQUIPMENT SET UP. HE SAY ANYTHING ABOUT A **TAPE**?

NO. HE DID SAY HE HAD EVIDENCE, THOUGH. I SUPPOSE THAT WOULD BE IT...

WHAT WILL HAPPEN TO VANCE? WILL HE... GO TO THE CUBES?

NO, HE'LL BE DISMISSED FROM THE FORCE. PROBABLY EXILED FROM THE CITY.

THEN I'LL GO WITH HIM! YES, WE'LL START AFRESH! IT WILL ALL BE SO DIFFERENT, NOT HAVING TO HIDE OUR LOVE! IN THE END, THIS WILL ALL HAVE BEEN FOR THE BEST.

CONTROL — THEY FIND ANY SIGN OF A TAPE SLUG IN THE FALUCCI CASE?

NEGATIVE. NOTHING ON THE BODY OR IN THE APARTMENT. SOMETHING INTERESTING, THOUGH —

FORENSIC TOOK A GENETIC SPECTROGRAM OF DANDRUFF FOUND ON FALUCCI'S BODY. IT BELONGS TO ONE **SONNY MOKOLINO**...

MOKOLINO JUST HAPPENS TO BE ONE OF THE CREEPS SLADEK WAS CHECKING ON BEFORE HE WENT ON SILENT.

THE **STIFF** HE LEFT US IS ONE OF MOKOLINO'S KNOWN ASSOCIATES.

DROKK! THEN THE MUGGERS MUST HAVE GOT THE FALUCCI TAPE — TRIED TO BLACKMAIL SLADEK. IT ALL FITS!

IS SOMETHING WRONG?

YEAH! YOUR BOYFRIEND MAY HAVE JUST LET LOVE GO TO HIS HEAD!

CONTROL! GOT ANY IDEA OF MOKOLINO'S WHEREABOUTS?

NO FIXED ABODE. KNOWN TO HANG OUT AT **MOPAD LO413**, CURRENTLY LOOPING THE SKED.

I'M HITTING THE SKED NOW. I'LL COVER THE MOPAD. GET UNITS TO ADDRESSES OF ALL KNOWN ASSOCIATES OF MOKOLINO. **WE GOT A POSSIBLE ROGUE JUDGE ON OUR HANDS!**

SO WHEN ME AN' KNEE HEARD THIS THUMP UP ON DECK, WE FIGURED IT WAS DIRTY JOHN. WE SHOULDA BEEN SO LUCKY.

CREMOLA! SLYDOG!

WHERE'S THE **TAPE**, DIRTBAG?

'COURSE, NOBODY TOOK NO NOTICE. I MEAN, JUDGE SHOOTIN' A JUVE — COULDN'T BE ANYTHIN' MORE NATURAL.

THE TAPE!

I-I'LL GET IT!

I DON'T KNOW WHAT YOU'RE— AHHHH!

KNEE!

IT WAS COLD-BLOODED MURDER. KNEE DIDN'T STAND A CHANCE.

BA!

I KNEW HE WAS GOING TO KILL ME TOO. I HAD TO DO SOMETHING...

HERE IT IS!

BUT WHEN I TRIED TO JUMP HIM...

BLAM!

STUPID PUNK!

P-PLEASE, JUDGE! YOU GOT THE SLUG! I WON'T TELL NOBODY!

DAMN RIGHT YOU WON'T!

FOR THE CRIMES OF MURDER AND BLACKMAIL I SENTENCE YOU TO —

SLADEK!

SPANG!

PUT 'EM ON, SLADEK. YOU'RE FINISHED!

DREDD

AN' THAT'S ABOUT IT, JUDGE DREDD.

WUP YAP

OKAY, MOKOLINO. YOU'LL BE GIVEN COPIES OF THIS STATEMENT TO SIGN. JUST A FORMALITY.

HEY, JUDGE. 25 YEARS IS A BIT STIFF. I BEEN STRAIGHT WITH YOU. ANY CHANCE OF A REDUC—?

FLAKE OFF!

"Woke up late today. I suppose it was staying so long at Pandrop's party. Pandrop had found a really good mess on the floor and we'd been eating it till the small hours.

"The gang were already up and about. I joined them for breakfast.

I ASSURE YOU, JUDGE DREDD, OUR KITCHEN IS CLEAN!

I'LL BE THE JUDGE OF THAT!

CRASH!

WHAT'S THIS — CLEAN-O-SPRA

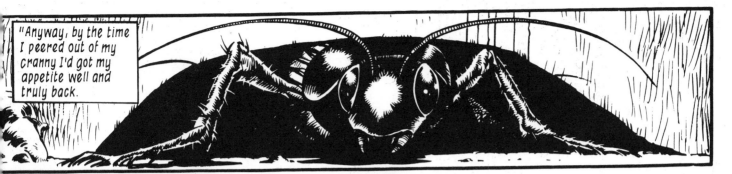

"Anyway, by the time I peered out of my cranny I'd got my appetite well and truly back."

"I'm 13½, which is quite old for a roach, so I'm big enough to make sure I always get the tastiest bits."

The Secret DIARY OF ADRIAN COCKROACH aged 13½ months

ER, Y-YES!

IT'S GREASE, CREEP!

WHAT KIND OF SOUP YOU MAKING, PAL — DANDRUFF?

GET A HAT ON!

GE DREDD

YOU - **NOSEPICK!** WAIT BY THE DOOR!

"I felt the vibration of approaching humans. Humans are our enemies. They don't understand us roaches."

SPLATT!

YOU OUGHT TO GO INTO THE **ROACH** BREEDING BUSINESS!

I'M CLOSING DOWN THIS **EATERIE**, PENDING HEALTH INSPECTION AND FUMIGATION.

AS FOR YOU, CREEP, YOU'RE DOING TIME.

THAT GOES FOR YOU TOO, NOSEPICK. **MOVE!**

"After all that excitement it was some time before I could summon up the courage to venture out. I'm not very brave by nature. More kind of **sly.**"

"I was still first to Renaldo and Sandra, though."

"There's not much room for sentiment in the roach world."

SLURP! SLURP!

YOU'VE DONE IT NOW, COOKIE! MY POP'S GOING TO THE CUBES AND IT'S **YOUR** FAULT!

**MY** FAULT?

WE TOLD YOU AND TOLD YOU! GET THIS KITCHEN CLEANED UP! GET RID OF THE ROACHES!

AN' I TOLD YOU TO GET A **ROBOT**! I'M NOT A PERISHING SKIVVY! I'M AN **EATERIE CHEF**! AN **ARTISTE**!

"My girlfriend Pandrop scuttled along and I let her share Sandra."

WELL GO BE AN ARTISTE SOMEWHERE ELSE! YOU'RE **FIRED**!

"Pandrop's got lovely legs — all six of them. She's the light of my life."

YOU YOUNG WHIPPERSNAPPER! I'VE BEEN COOKING IN THIS EATERIE TWENTY YEARS!

I'LL GIVE YOU FIRED!

NO—!

CREMOLA — YOU KILLED 'IM, COOKIE!

I-I GOTTA CALL THE JUDGES!

"I'm always alert for danger. I guess that's why I've stayed alive so long."

"Deep down in the woodwork is my secret, gasproof bunker. There I stayed all day long."

"When I eventually crept out, it was to a scene of utter devastation. I was the **only** survivor."

"And woe! Even Pandrop—my dear sweet Pandrop—lay legs up and lifeless."

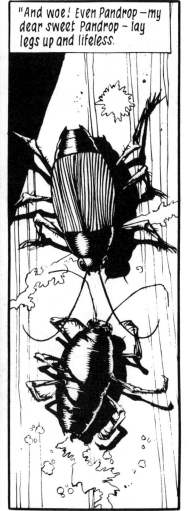

"Oh, well. Like I said, there's no room for sentiment in the roach world. Pandrop and I dined together for the last time."

"And so to bed...

" ...wonder what tomorrow will bring?"

THE END.

SAP WAS DOWN FOR A SIMPLE ARM FRACTURE. THAT WOULD MAKE MY 834TH. YOU MIGHT SAY I'M GETTIN' TO BE A BIT OF A **BONE SPECIALIST**.

YES? WHAT DO YOU WANT?

THE NAME'S **MARLOWE**. I'M A **PRIVATE EYE**.

THE "EYE" STANDS FOR **INTIMIDATOR**. THAT'S MY JOB. INTIMIDATIONS CARRIED OUT, DISCRETION GUARANTEED.

**NUHHHHH!**

NUHHH YOURSELF, SCUMBO!

101 L

THE JOB ON HIS NOSE WASN'T WHAT I WAS BEIN' PAID FOR. STILL, I COULD AFFORD TO THROW IT IN FOR FREE. I LIKE TO DO A SERVICE.

**AAAAH!**

101 L

THE MESSAGE IS "PAY UP BY THURSDAY, LOUIE, OR NEXT TIME IT'S **THE BIG SLEEP**".

THAT MEAN ANYTHING TO YOU, PAL?

SURE! IT MEANS YOU'RE AN IDIOT! I AIN'T LOUIE — LOUIE LIVES NEXT DOOR!

CORRECTION, CONTROL! THIS LOOKS LIKE **MURDER**.

SEND DOWN A FORENSIC SQUAD. AM INVESTIGATING.

NOBODY LASTS LONG IN THIS GAME MAKING MISTAKES —

—AND I'D JUST MADE TWO...

BLOOD!

HEADING TOWARDS THE HOVER PORT!

YOU! HOLD IT!

BLAM

# THE BIG SLEEP: DREDD MAKES NOVEL ARREST!

I LOST THEM IN THE PEDWAYS UNDER THE INTERSECT.

I KNEW WHAT I HAD TO DO AND I KNEW I HAD TO DO IT FAST. I WAS PRACTICALLY BAILING BLOOD FROM THE POD.

WE'VE LOST CONTACT!

I FIGURED I HAD MAYBE TEN MINUTES LEFT BEFORE *THE BIG SLEEP*.

AT **DONALD NEIL BLOCK** —

CONTROL HERE, DREDD. CREEP WAS REAL TRICKY. H-WAGON LOST HIM.

BETTER PUT OUT AN **APB**, CONTROL. ALERT THE HOSPITALS. HE WAS WOUNDED. HE'LL NEED HELP.

YOU GET A GOOD LOOK AT YOUR ATTACKER, CITIZEN?

N-NO. I WAS TOO BUSY GETTIN' MY BONES BROKE. HE... HE WAS WEARING A POD SUIT — WITH ONE OF THOSE PIG HELMETS.

HE READ OUT THIS MESSAGE — "PAY UP BY THURSDAY, LOUIE"...

...I TOLD HIM, I AIN'T LOUIE. LOUIE LIVES NEXT DOOR. HE DIDN'T SEEM TO **CARE** WHAT HE'D DONE TO ME!

HIRED MUSCLE, I'D SAY – AND NOT VERY SMART MUSCLE AT THAT.

YOU WERE LUCKY TO GET AWAY WITH YOUR LIFE. FOR THE RIGHT PRICE SCUM LIKE HIM WILL DO ANYTHING – TO ANYBODY.

QUESTION IS, WHAT DID YOUR NEIGHBOUR DO TO EARN A VISIT FROM A PRIVATE INTIMIDATOR?

I FIGURED I'D DROP IN ON HERRY UNEXPECTED, JUST IN CASE HE HAD ANY MORE MOVES UP HIS SLEEVE –

CRRRASHH!

AAAH!

YOU SET ME UP, DIDN'T YOU, HERRY?

ME? DON'T BE CRAZY! I AIN'T JUST YOUR AGENT – I'M YOUR PAL! I WOULDN'T SEND YOU ON NO SLEEPWALK!

DON'T LIE TO ME! IT HAD TO BE YOU!

THUD! THUD! THUD!

BOZO WAS **WAITIN'** FOR ME WITH AN ARSENAL! **YOU** BOOKED ME THE JOB, HERRY! **YOU** WERE THE ONLY ONE KNEW WHEN I WAS GONNA BE THERE.

IT—IT'S NOT TRUE! YOU GOTTA BELIEVE ME, FLIP!

BALL'S IN YOUR COURT, HERRY! I STOP BANGING WHEN YOU STOP LYIN'!

THUNGG! THUNGG!

ALL RIGHT! FOR MERCY'S SAKE —

SO I DID SET YOU UP. I HAD MY REASONS. YOU WERE GETTIN' TOO HARD TO CONTROL, FLIP. TOO RECKLESS. YOU WERE MAKING MISTAKES AND THAT'S BAD.

**MAKING MISTAKES... I COULDN'T ARGUE WITH THAT. I TOLD HIM ABOUT BREAKING THE WRONG GUY'S ARM...**

SEE WHAT I MEAN, FLIP? YOU'RE OVER THE HILL. YOU'RE A DANGER TO ALL OF US. THAT'S WHY I HAD TO DO IT.

YOU UNDERSTAND THAT, DON'T YOU, FLIP?

AAAAGH!

SURE, HERRY, I UNDERSTAND.

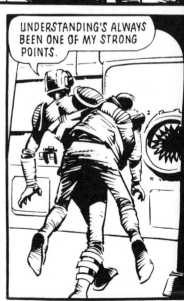

UNDERSTANDING'S ALWAYS BEEN ONE OF MY STRONG POINTS.

AND A GUY WHO LOVES HIS RAT CAN'T BE ALL BAD.

FAAPOOOM

CONTROL TO DREDD! WE JUST DUG ONE **FLIP MARLOWE** OUT OF A POD SMASH ON THE *SKED*. HE'S GOT TWO OF YOUR BULLETS IN HIM.

THAT'S THE **NEIL BLOCK KILLER**. SEE IF YOU CAN GET ANY LEADS ON WHO HIRED HIM.

ANY POINT ME COMING OVER?

NOT UNLESS YOU WANT TO SEE A GOOD MESS. CREEP BROKE EVERY BONE IN HIS BODY.

NO MORE THAN HE DESERVED.

THE END.